LOVE, SEX, AND MONEY

THE KEYS TO HAVING A SUCCESSFUL MARRIAGE

DR. DAPHNE MCKENZIE MCNISH

ISBN: 978-1-948777-26-1

Printed in the United States of America

CONTENTS

Acknowledgments   v

Introduction   vii

Chapter 1   1
HAPPY EVER AFTER

Chapter 2   4
MONEY IS NOT THE FIRST PRIORITY

Chapter 3   9
LOVE FLOWS FREELY FROM THE HEART

Chapter 4   13
I AM NOT YOUR MOTHER

Chapter 5   17
I AM NOT YOUR EX!

Chapter 6   21
I AM TOO TIRED

Chapter 7   25
BE SUBMISSIVE

Chapter 8   29
DATE NIGHT

Chapter 9   34
FOREPLAY

Chapter 10   37
MY HEAD HURTS!

The Bestsellers Academy   43

ACKNOWLEDGMENTS

To the Holy Spirit, thank you for speaking to my soul, reminding me what you have taught me by conducting pre-marital and marital counseling, and reminding me of what the world needs to know. Thank you for entrusting me with the secrets to marriage so your people can enjoy their marriage without thinking of divorce. To my heavenly Father, I am eternally grateful to you for using one like me to write this book, O Lord my God, thou art very great; Thou art clothed with honor and majesty. To my loving husband Charles McNish, thank you for believing in me. I am still desperately in love with you after all these years. To my son Phillip, I thank God for you. My two sisters, Lissa and Sylvia, my nieces, Kerry-Ann and Beulah, I love you all. I appreciate you Dionne Poyser. Thank you for your encouragement. I am so happy to know you are people that love God with all of your hearts. To my stepdaughter who keeps telling me I can do it, thank you. I love and appreciate all of you, even when I am feeling like giving up. Because of your faith in me, I keep on writing. I am blessed to be a part of our family. To *Plan A Global* for all your encouragements and prayers, thank you so much. May God continue to strengthen all eagles' wings so they can fly to the height God will have them to go. Thanks again, people of God.

INTRODUCTION

My name is Dr. Daphne McKenzie McNish. I have been married for 18 years, but I am not a marriage expert by any means. As a minister, I found myself counseling married and engaged couples. Through that process, I learned so much about the things that would throw them into a big fuss without even thinking, and how so many couples did not know how to fight fair. I was amazed by how God used (and still using me) to counsel couples with great results. I can say I learned a lot from this to help make my own marriage stronger. I am thankful to the Almighty God for anointing me for such a task.

This is the first and only publication of this kind about marriage. Let me explain, there are many books about marriage; however, they do not get to the real meat of the matter.

Too many marriages have been very unhappy, even to the point of divorce, because they do not understand how to deal with issues in their relationships. The goal of this book is to change the entire way you look at your marriage, learning to appreciate and love each other in a new way. If you are reading this book, I believe your marriage will become stronger. Let's see what the Bible says:

So the LORD God caused the man to fall into a deep sleep; and while he was sleeping, he took one of the man's ribs and then closed up the place with flesh. Then the LORD God made a woman from the rib he had taken out of the man, and he brought her to the man. The man said, "This is now bone of my bone and flesh of my flesh; she shall be called 'woman,' for she was taken out of man." That is why a man leaves his father and mother and is united to his wife, and they become one flesh. (Genesis 2:21-24, NIV)

It is for these reasons, and by the grace of God, that this book will gain worldwide readership. Marriage is holy and was ordained by God; we should never take it lightly. I pray that by reading this book you will be motivated to apply some, if not all, of these principles, enjoy reading, enjoy your marriage to the fullest, and love God with all your heart, putting God first. This book, *Love, Sex, and Money,* is a book that will open your eyes to some the things you think are not important to your marriage. May God help you to understand this book in the way He wants you to.

CHAPTER ONE
HAPPY EVER AFTER

AND THEY LIVE HAPPILY EVER AFTER, yeah, sure. In fairy tales, maybe. Or in your dreams. Many of us ladies had been thinking about marriage since we were little girls; we were expecting our prince to come on a beautiful white horse to sweep us off our feet. But ladies, I am sorry, it does not work like that! You have got to wake up and come to reality; this is the real world. Some of us get married and then once we realize that our husbands are not the princes we think they should be, we want to leave and go back to mommy. When we are married, that should never be our first option. There is always wisdom in God's words, and there are always people who can help.

One thing we must remember is that there is no perfect mate; that is a *myth*. For example, a woman might complain that her husband never tells her that he loves her, except on her birthday and when he asked her to marry him. He has been bringing her flowers every weekend but never says a word, so she is not convinced of his love. She does not yet understand that most men, no matter how brave they are, are not verbal, preferring instead to speak with actions—and there is nothing wrong with that! She got so worked up for nothing.

I am pleading to ladies not to be so insecure. When you are insecure, you see everything differently and make yourself unhappy. We ladies must be confident in everything we do. We are uniquely made, out of the rib of our husbands. There are lots of ways your husband can tell you that he loves you without speaking. The way he looks at you, the tender way he holds you, even the tone in his voice can tell you that this man is in love with you. And I am not talking about sex or getting lots of gifts; do not mistake sex and gifts for love—yes, they are very important in a marriage, but don't be fooled. Remember, gifts are just things.

But love is not something you turn on and off when you feel like it. Love is not a feeling. It cannot be turned off because you feel you should punish your spouse. Real love flows freely from the heart. To me, love is like a spring of fresh clean water flowing freely from the top of a mountain, bubbling over all different kinds of rocks and plants to the bottom of the mountain where everyone has the privilege to drink from it. Some catch this water in a bottle and keep it sealed. Some catch it and try to give it to someone who they think would appreciate it. Some give it to someone, hoping that person would keep it and protect it but instead tramples on it without a care. Some think it's not for them, some think it's just an idea, it's not real. But everyone who ever has an encounter with this spring acts differently. Some get so bubbly with this water while others cannot understand.

I will give a word of caution: always make sure you go to God before you tell someone you love them. I am telling you there are people who will trample on your heart without even thinking twice and laugh in your face. Not everyone will be ready for the kind of love you have to share. Some might be very afraid and run for the hills, and yet, you have just the right person waiting to receive this love.

Do not be dismayed. Our God is an awesome God, all we have to do is depend on Him. He said, "Call and I will answer," (Psalm 91:15, NIV). He is the one that ordained marriage in the first place. He will work on the desire of our hearts (Psalm 37:4-5, NIV). We cannot be afraid to go to our Heavenly Father with any and everything. Love is a beautiful thing; everyone deserves to experience this beautiful love God made for us with the right person.

The Bible says, "Love is patient, love is kind. It does not dishonor others, it is not self-seeking, it is not easily angered, it keeps no record of wrongs" (1 Corinthians 13:4, NIV). Love in your marriage is of the utmost importance. Your marriage should be composed of friendship, sexual attraction, and accountability, but most importantly, your love. We must be committed to our marriage and do our part. Falling in love seems easy at times, but keeping your marriage strong will take ongoing work. We must be compassionate to each other and protect each other. The good news is that marriage is built on Christ the solid rock. He is always there to help us when we call. Please remember love honors God. Do not deprive yourself of this wonderful gift.

Because love is real and it is from God, we must keep our eyes open. Sometimes we get too comfortable or lazy and forget the enemy is waiting and lurking around to attack our marriage. We must be fully armed at all times, like soldiers, we must be ready to fight for our marriage. We cannot be careless, we must be relentless; we will always win. Remember we never fight alone, but we must do our part. Our Heavenly Father Abba is always in our battle and He never lost a fight, so never give up on your marriage. Continue to love each other and keep on fighting.

CHAPTER TWO
MONEY IS NOT THE FIRST PRIORITY

SOME OF YOU might remember when ladies were expected to get married and be housewives and mothers, supported financially by their husbands back in the 1950s-1970s. Things have changed since then! Some of us don't mind if our husbands take care of us financially, but in other aspects, especially the area of communication, we wish they would, let me say—be more like us ladies. Listen ladies, this will never be.

Men speak a different language than we do; we will talk about that later. But back to the issue of money, imagine your friend complains that her husband is not making enough money to meet her needs and this makes her frustrated. Your friend knows the kind of job her husband does; she knows he's not a rich man. When they first met she got so caught up in dating and didn't ask the right questions, and he didn't feel like he should volunteer any information about his salary. Now he has been at the same job since they met, and despite his recent promotion, she is unhappy. Let me say this, some of us ladies don't understand how depressed and sad it can be when a husband finds himself in a position where he can't take care of his family; we don't know the pain they go through and how embarrassed they can get. This is when we should take time out to know them, to understand and love them and not beat them down.

In some marriages, money is the top priority, not love, and this can make or break a marriage. Don't get me wrong, there is nothing wrong with money! Our heavenly Father Abba wants us to have money, we cannot live without it. Remember Abba is the one who made all things, all diamonds, rubies, and all precious stones for us to enjoy and to give to worthy kingdom causes, remembering the orphans and widows, and not putting it above our Heavenly Father Abba, He must be first at all times. The scripture says about money as our number one priority, "The love of money is the root of all kinds of evil. Some people, eager for money, have wandered from the faith and pierced themselves with many griefs" (1 Timothy 6:10 NIV).

Sometimes in marriage money can become a stumbling block. We must be very careful not to endanger our marriage because of it. Yes, money can buy a beautiful house, but it cannot buy a home. It can buy people, but not love; it can buy medicine, but not good health.

Before marriage, money should be discussed to avoid any potential misunderstanding. If you both have a problem discussing money, then seek a financial adviser to help you. Money must never be a power play in your marriage; you and your spouse must never feel like you are in a competition in any way. You are a team, and so you must work as a team.

On the other hand, there are men who do not know how to take care of their family—some because of their association with certain kinds of people, and others due to what was modeled for them in their households as children. But whatever the reason, a husband and father must do what men are supposed to do, which is to take care of his family—to stand up for them and be their leader.

Remember, having children does not make someone a man,

liking the idea of being married does not make someone a man; it is not about wearing a ring or being in control. It is about a man loving his family and taking care of them; that is the role of a husband. God put him as the head of the household not to be a taskmaster over his family, but to love and protect them.

At the same time, a wife must respect her husband as the head of their home. It does not matter what she thinks; this is God's law. We will explore that in a later chapter. The Bible has this to say about the dynamic between a husband and wife: "Husbands, in the same way, be considerate as you live with your wives, and treat them with respect as the weaker vessel and as heirs with you of the gracious gift of life, so that nothing will hinder your prayers" (1 Peter 3:7, NIV).

Husbands sometimes want their wives to respect their direction in life, even if they do not fully understand or stand in agreement with his vision. It is really amazing that even when a man is not doing the right thing, he is expecting his wife to respect him, and rightly so, because they were born this way. And the Bible tells us as wives to respect our husbands; there is no getting around it. And husbands, notice Job, when his wife told him to curse God and die, what did he say? He said, "You speak like a foolish woman" (Job 2:10, NIV), but he did not call her foolish. This tells me Job knew his wife was not foolish, only speaking without thinking. I think he knew she was suffering as much as he was, and she was angry, and I think she was very misunderstood.

Husbands, take care of your wives and do not mistreat them in any way. Let's get back to money.

Sad to say some spouses are in big trouble when it comes to money. There should be no competition in marriage with money or anything else. In some marriages, the husbands become resentful if their wives are making more money than they do. This should never be so. We should be happy for each other and applaud our partner in everything they do.

Wives, so many of you have shared this secret with me. It was disturbing for me to hear it, and it needs to be talked about. There are some husbands that will give their wives money for housekeeping, but never follow up. They just expect the bills to be paid, and the refrigerator to be full, yet they never ask how much the bills and groceries cost each month, leaving all that stress on their wives. Some wives are afraid to bring it up, so they find themselves borrowing from Peter to pay Paul, as one would say. This could mean there will always be unpaid bills, or bills in the back.

Now this becomes the elephant in the room. If a wife is working and can help, that's one situation, but a stay-at-home mom will be in trouble not knowing what to do. Ephesians 5:28, NIV tells us that "husbands ought to love their wives as their own bodies. So, he who loves his wife loves himself." Notice the emphasis of headship is not based upon power or control, but upon love and care. There should never be selfish demands placed on each other.

Another thing wives have told me is that they are saddened by the way their husbands act at times, when they see their wives getting something new, such as a new phone. Their husbands think they have the right, or they feel they deserve the same things. Some husbands might even take the item and never use it. They say sometimes even if they need to replace a broken phone, their husbands feel they should get a new one too, even if he really doesn't need it. But the scripture reminds us what jealousy and envy can do. The biblical difference between them is that jealousy can be a positive thing sometimes, but envy is never positive; it is always negative. Genesis 4:1-8, NIV tells us how Cain envied his brother Abel, and it became murder. Envy is dangerous, and it is a spirit that cannot stay in your marriage. It has no place in your marriage. We must be happy for each other and want the best for our partner at all times.

In marriage each of us must first grow as an individual before we can grow together as a couple. We must become each other's biggest cheerleader and be careful not to let anyone take that place.

It is a great feeling just to know your lover is always cheering you on. They stand by you no matter what, in your bad times and your good times. What a great blessing God has provided for us from before the foundation of this world! To Him be all Honor and glory.

CHAPTER THREE
LOVE FLOWS FREELY FROM THE HEART

ONE OF MY clients used to complain about her husband always leaving the toilet seat up, and how very annoying it was when he put the toilet paper on the holder the wrong way, not to her standard. Listen wives, love does not come with conditions; if you want your home to be happy you and your partner cannot pick at every little thing each other does. None of us is made perfect yet.

And yes, I get it, but men do not think anything of this! They do not even know these things bother, things like putting the toilet paper on the holder the "wrong way," not to our liking. But look at it this way: they did make sure to replace the toilet paper! Everything is well with the world, and we are getting steamed up. Remember wives, this home is their home too; they do not have to be walking on eggshells in their home. Wives, I get it. You just cleaned the house yesterday, but your husband seems to put things … let me say, *not* where you would want them to be. But you have to strategically find a way to help him without making him feel bad. You know him more than anyone else; you can do this.

And yes, our homes should be clean and a haven of comfort and peace, not a den of worry. This will make our husbands spend time with people they can be comfortable around, so you might wonder, *why is he spending so much time at his mother's house or with his friends?* Maybe you cannot understand why, but these are places where he feels the most freedom, and maybe those surroundings might be cleaner than his home. Wives, this is a part of your responsibility as a wife. Not all husbands know how to clean up, but we can teach them if they are willing to learn.

Now he is not spending enough time with you, and you are feeling paranoid about his actions. Maybe you're nagging. This can put either one of you out of the marital home, and it should not be so. According to (1 Corinthians 13:4- 5), "Love is patient, love is kind. It does not envy, it does not boast, it is not proud. It does not dishonor others, it is not self-seeking, it is not easily angered, it keeps no record of wrongs." We should always remember this. God will hold us guilty for the way we treat each other. Please be mindful that marriage was made by God and it is holy.

We cannot always do as we feel. There are spiritual laws that go along with marriage and if a couple does not heed them, their marriage will be in trouble. We can never do marriage on our own, we will never win. Marriage can be hard if you don't depend on God. One thing you must never do is to be a nagging wife; that can turn your husband off badly: "Better to live in a desert, than with a quarrelsome and nagging wife" (Proverbs 21:19, NIV).

Nagging makes you depressed and can stop you from sleeping and eating. It can get to the point where you are not taking care of your home and aren't acting like yourself anymore, your whole world becomes dark. Let me say this, nagging has no gender. Some spouses don't even understand what is going on with their partner, because they become so distant and keep everything inside.

It is unhealthy for any marriage to be filled with criticism and nagging. This will not bring your spouse any closer; instead it will drive them away. Find more effective ways to communicate in your relationship and leave the nagging behind. Nagging is irritating, frustrating, and annoying.

Spouses have no legitimate excuse for nagging each other. We often think our spouses have problems and it is up to us to fix them. This is wrong. We need fixing ourselves. We must try not to manipulate our spouse. We should always try to find a way to make our spouse happy, then the whole family will be happy. If you are a nagging spouse you will need some help to find out what is really going on; there is always something else at the bottom of it. Everything negative will have to go so that this marriage can move on.

When you are mad at the world or anyone else, you should never try to take it out on your spouse and make them feel it was their fault. Your spouse should not be your enemy, but your safe place. When your spouse feels safe, they will relax and open their hearts, and there is no need to force intimacy or any kind of connection.

Let me say, our heavenly Father Abba made us as His masterpiece, and gave us wonderful hearts that should be open. We lose lots of energy with a closed heart. What a waste of time!

We must never play the blame game with each other; every problem must be solved in love. We must learn to listen to our spouse; we do not have to be the one talking at all times, listening can be every effective. Do not let little things fester in your mind. They will become huge and before you know, it's out of control. Let them go.

After we have been married for a year or so, many of us forget to say please and thank you, to show our appreciation for each other. We should not be taking each other for granted! This we should never push to the side. Sometimes we do not even value our spouse's opinions anymore. This is sad! There is hardly any communication, you stop exchanging text messages, stop telling each other how you feel about each other, stop putting love notes around the house like you used to. Not doing these things anymore, the little ways you used to show love and affection early on, can certainly put a wedge between you. I pray you may ask God to open your eyes and give you wisdom to avoid anything that will drive a wedge between you and your partner. Your love for each other must keep burning in the mighty name of Jesus.

ONE OF MY girlfriends came to see me about a problem she was having in her marriage. Her husband did not enjoy the meals she prepared in their home because they did not taste like his mother's. He wanted her to go to his mother's house for cooking lessons. He constantly complained that she did not do things the way his mother did; everything she did should be like his mommy. She was getting tired of this, and wanted to tell him, "Move back to your mommy, then, so I don't slap you like your mommy did when you were a boy!"

Husbands, your wife is not your mother! As Rick Joyner often states in his book *The Seer*, there are no two snowflakes that are alike! Genesis 2:22-24, NIV reads, "Then the Lord God made a woman from the rib he had taken out of the man, and he brought her to the man. The man said, 'this is now bone of my bones and flesh of my flesh; she shall be called woman, for she was taken out of man.'" That is why a man leaves his father and mother and is united to his wife, and they become one flesh.

Grow up and be a man, stop treating your wife like your mother! She does not have to cook like your mother, she is her own independent individual, and you can't turn her into your mother. Ladies, as his wife be sure to tell him that you cannot replace his mother.

I must tell you ladies, unfortunately some men go around looking for women that look like their mothers. These men will act like children, but this does not mean you must treat them like children. Look, in every man there is a little boy somewhere inside, but unfortunately some of them are still immature. It is not your responsibility to treat your husband like a son; you are his wife, and he must be reminded that you do not want to be his mother! Love for your mother is one thing, but love for your wife is another thing. Do not mix them up; learn the difference.

As mothers, we love our sons, but we have to let them fly. They will always love us and nothing can stop that—keep in mind that your son's wife could be a mother to a son tomorrow! We must be on our guard not to step in our children's romantic relationships, we just might make a big mess.

This is why both parties should try to learn as much as they can about each other before saying "I do." This is hardball, and you must be ready. Dating can be kind of a fairy tale we get caught up in, and we might forget about everything else.

There are a lot of things you will not know about your spouse, even after five years—not because there is something to hide, but sometimes it takes a while for the dating mask to eventually peel off. This is how we really start getting to know each other. This is one of the reasons why you must be very sure both of you want to be married.

Ask yourself questions like, *Am I going to be able to embrace another person's weaknesses and remember they are human? Am I comfortable with another person decorating, or changing things around in the house I call my own? Am I willing to share my house and make it a home for my new family? Am I willing to invest in marriage now? Can I deal with in-laws? Am I in a good place for marriage, or do I need to stay at my mother's house a while longer?* These are just some of the questions we need to answer for ourselves. When these questions are not answered before marriage, then later in marriage there can be problems.

It can be very sad when problems like illness or other troubles occur in some marriages and the spouses begin to treat each other like strangers. Therefore, we must go to God in prayer and fasting; He will tell us what to do. We must develop a strong relationship with our Heavenly Father so we can hear when He speaks. He spoke to men of old, and He is still speaking today. He never gives bad gifts, and He is waiting on us to come to Him. He is a good and loving Father who takes care of His children.

We cannot spend a lot of time blaming each other when we should be calling out to our heavenly father Abba for help as a team. We must join forces against the enemy, and not our spouse. It does not matter how things might look; only God is the answer to any problems we may come across.

Marriage will be always under attack by the enemy as long as this world lasts. This is why we must make sure you are ready for this kind of battle. But our Father has never lost a battle! This should make you want to skip and jump, knowing who God is.

Let me remind some wives that sometimes after we have been married, we turn our husbands off by not taking care of ourselves anymore. We think we don't need to because we are already married, but this not right, and it is selfish. Your spouse wants to see you the way he met you. We must be able to go on the street the way we are dressed at home.

If your spouse should call to let you know he is stopping by with a friend, you should not have to tell him to reschedule for another day—the home should be clean at all times. Stay the kind of loving, caring, bubbly person you were before you got married. Once you make a change in your character there will be trouble; this might indicate that you were wearing different masks and cannot be trusted. This is why it is best to be ourselves at all times. It does not matter who you are; you are unique the way God made you, and you do not have to change for anyone.

Apostle Renatah Henderson is the founder and teacher of Plan A Global, a fivefold ministry school that I am attending. She is my mentor, and one of the most important lessons she taught me was that we are whom God says we are, and so we have nothing to prove, nothing to hide, nothing to defend, or nothing to protect. So when we really know who we are, we should be comfortable in our own skin as a child of God. You don't have to live in someone else's shadow; God has given you your own unique space, and no one can be like you. You are your Heavenly Father Abba's master-piece, you are uniquely made with your own personality, so be happy with who you are and be you, in every meaning of the word. No one can take that away from you. Be all that God will have you to be, in Jesus's name.

CHAPTER FIVE
I AM NOT YOUR EX!

"WHY ARE you treating me like your ex?" my cousin Calvin complained to his wife. His wife had gone through a nasty divorce six years ago and he thought she had gotten over it. They dated for two years and everything was fine, but now that they are married he says that all hell has broken loose—everything and anything he does or says seems to not be up to her standard and she tells him, "You are just like my ex." He told me that he does not know what to do at this point.

Well, this is what I told Calvin: Some people try to get away from their past relationship by getting into another, but this is not the solution. The first relationship must completely come to a close before you can move on.

She will need some help through counseling to learn how to break away from her past before she can move on. Premarital counseling is so important! You must never go into someone life with all your baggage—this will pull them down, and it is not fair. This marriage will not be happy without a whole lot of work, but they must be willing to do the work. We must be honest when we meet someone and we see things are getting serious. Sometimes there are warning signs, but we do not take the time to see them until it's too late. For example, every time you are on a date the ex-husband or wife name's would come up more than once, talking about the food they liked, and places they liked to go, things they liked to do. Sometimes they even want you to be dress like their ex, or they try to find someone with the same name as their ex, that kind of thing. This can be linked to obsession, or sometimes the person might even need deliverance.

It is very important to know what you are getting into. You don't have to be trapped in this, the huge red flag is in your face. Unfortunately, some will dive right in, believing they can fix the person and by time they are done, they will forget their ex and just concentrate on them.

You are making the biggest mistake of your life; you cannot fix anyone or make them just for you. You are not God! I can tell you that you will be trapped, and this will be a disaster waiting to happen. We can't play with each other's lives; humans are not toys. It is okay to be sad after a breakup; you are human and must give yourself time to grieve and then move on and not be a victim. It is just an experience that will help you along your life's journey, and I know this is hard to do but you must forgive and move on; you cannot be a victim for the rest of your life.

The Bible tells us in Matthew 5:44, NIV to love our enemies and to pray for those who persecute us, and I can tell you the word of God works. My advice is to also encourage your wife to let God transform her by His words; as Romans 12:2 says, "Do not conform to the pattern of this world, but be transformed by the renewing of your mind. Then you will be able to test and approve what God's will is—His good, pleasing and perfect will" (NIV). These are God's words and we must obey them; otherwise, we are heading for destruction. Remember the enemy will play tricks in your mind, so you must be on guard. If you don't, it will control your mind completely and you will lose yourself.

We must speak the truth; our lives will be so much happier. How can you say you love me and you can't tell me what is in your heart? Does this mean you do not trust me with your heart?

We are our own people coming from different backgrounds, so how did we get here? This is why we should always do our research when we find ourselves falling in love and think we are ready for the step of marriage. We must look into our families' backgrounds to see what kind of diseases, if any, are in the family line, and what kind of generational curses, if any, might be in the family line. This is not to put each other down, but for you both to be in deep prayer and fasting to break these curses so your marriage will be free. This cannot be a one-time thing.

Let me remind you, this is Biblical. This is just one of many scriptures:

> *You shall not bow down to them or worship them; for I, the LORD your God, am a jealous God, punishing the children for the sin of the parents to the third and fourth generation of those who hate me, but showing love to a thousand generations of those who love me and keep my commandments.* (Exodus 20:5-6, NIV).

We don't know what our ancestors were doing back then: what god or gods they were worshipping, what kind of lives they were living, maybe never repenting. This is very important to know, so we must be careful not to open any doors, and there will be less stress in your marriage, so we can be free to love.

Because love comes freely from the heart, and it is real, you should want to take care of each other the best way you can. Never assume you know what your partner is going to say or do, and never jump to conclusions about your spouse; this will turn them off completely. Never put words in your spouse's mouth; this is trouble, and it is not worth it. Learn to appreciate your spouse for who he or she is, not who you think they should be. They are God's creation, wonderfully made in his own image. Again, God will hold us guilty.

Your spouse must be able to speak their mind and not be judged. It is your responsibility to your spouse to let them know and feel you really care for them and everything related to them because they are a part of you. We are one and should hurt for each other.

In our marriage we will always mess up, but we can ask our spouse's forgiveness and move on. We have to remember, we are human without perfection, and our marriage is a blessing, God's incredible gift to us. I pray we would take our marriage seriously the way God wants us to do. Then we will see the love of God through our spouse's eyes.

Do not expect it will be sunshine and roses every day, but it should not be hell on earth! Learn to fight well, not hard. Speak well about your spouse to others; everyone likes to feel appreciated. For example, say something nice about your spouse in the presence of their parents or friends. Someone will be sure to tell your spouse and you will be credited. How about that!

CHAPTER SIX
I AM TOO TIRED

ONE OF MY CLIENTS, David, had a problem with his wife telling him every evening she was too tired to even have a conversation. David wondered why she was so tired, because she is at home every day; he just could not understand it. He must have forgotten they had three young children, ages six, four, and eight months, and a home to take care of.

When I spoke to his wife Rose, she told me he goes to work every morning by eight and she is already up fixing his breakfast, getting the two older children ready for school, and taking them to the bus stop, holding the baby in her arms. When she returns home after the kids are safely on the bus, she has to get something to eat, take care of the baby, put baby down for a nap, clean up the kitchen, take something out for dinner, take care of the baby after the nap, feed the baby, and put clothes in the washer (with the baby in hand). Now it's two in the afternoon: time to make the beds (with baby whining) and feed the baby. Now it's 3 p.m.: time to go to the bus stop. One child is here, now they wait for the other bus. Now it's 4 p.m., time to listen to everything that happened in school, give the kids snacks, and fix dinner while they watch TV. After dinner it is time for homework, then their shower and bedtime story. By now it's 8 p.m. already. David comes home, kisses the kids good night, eats his dinner, watches some TV, takes his shower, and goes to bed. Rose takes her shower and goes to bed, exhausted—and this is every day! And this was my advice to Rose: let him have a day with the kids and you take the day off, and it has to be a school day.

David's vacation comes around, and Rose made arrangements with her girlfriends and her sisters to have a day out. David was fine with it, he wanted to spent time with his kids. He planned to cook dinner for that night, thinking, *this should be so easy!* Rose left the house at 8 a.m. and made sure not to take her phone with her. At 11, he called her but soon found out she did not have her phone. At 7 that evening, Rose came home to a disaster! Nothing was done, not even dinner! She got home in time to get the kids to bed, and then she and David ordered dinner and had a good evening.

We must be careful not to assume things about our spouse; we must get to know them. Try to know why he or she gets so tired and fix it however you can. Get involved in whatever is going on in the home. Marriage is not actually 50/50, it is a 100/100 deal. We must be willing to surrender our all to each other. We are in this together and we must stand together. The kids belong to both of us, this is not a one man show. We must take the strain off each other. There are no special duties in the home for either one; it just depends on what you can do and are willing to do.

The Bible says in Amos 3:3, NIV, "Do two walk together unless they have agreed to do so?" Marriage needs two people to participate in everything for it to work. We should feel free and willing to help in our home to make it comfortable. It does not matter if your wife works outside the home or not; being a housewife is a full-time job, and with children, it is like two or more full-time jobs. Taking care of children and the home can be very stressful without help—it does not matter how organized she is. Husbands, you are responsible for helping to promote harmony in the home. Remember, husbands, it is your home too, and you need to help keep it clean. If you cook you are eating too. You should help with the kids because this is your job as their dad. Husbands, you are not the help in the home, you are a part of the home. Praise your wives in the same way, with intensity. Help around the house, behave like true husbands should in their home. You are not a guest in a hotel, feel at home and be at home, it is your home and family, God has given them to you.

When we have kids, they tend to keep their eyes on us, and they pick up on everything we say or do. You must remember, God loves family, and the children belong to him. You are the caretakers, so you must teach them godly values, teach them the word of God, write the promises of God and put them all over the house and remind them of His promises. Fill your home with praise and worship, and as a family you must pray together; the kids must see biblical love and principles in the home. Children are gifts from God. Proverbs 22:6, NIV says, "Start children off on the way they should go, and even when they are old, they will not turn from it". Biblical principles will help them with their families as well. Your background, culture, or social status does not matter; the biblical principles should be effective in our lives. They are God's laws for us.

Another thing we must talk about is spending a lot of time with your family. Before you know, your children will be grown and have their own lives. We must never neglect our family for anyone or anything, expect in very rare emergency cases where it cannot be avoided. You will never regret making memories that you can later share with your grandkids.

There are people who say it is not possible to have a happy marriage. Do not believe them; this is not true! "We can do all things through Christ who strengthens us" (Philippians 4:13, NIV). He is the one who created marriage in the first place, so I encourage you today, when you are in trouble, to go to Him and He will fix it.

Do not go to a divorce lawyer; God never intended for us to divorce. Keep your marriage God's way, until death do us part. Sometimes we do things with good intentions and it turns out wrong, and our spouses do not understand, but God does. Do not rush to judge each other, try to understand.

I will say this, whether you've been married for years or just got married recently, there is lots of work to be done for us to get to that happy place—but we can get there with the help of God. Trust Him to lead the way and just follow Him; you will get to that happy place and stay there, and nothing can move you, in Jesus's name.

CHAPTER SEVEN
BE SUBMISSIVE

THE SCRIPTURE SAYS,

Submit to one another out of reverence for Christ. Wives, submit yourselves to your own husband as you do to the Lord. For the husband is the head of the wife as Christ is the head of the church; his body, of which he is the Savior. Now as the church submits to Christ, so also wives should submit to their husbands in everything. (Ephesians 5:21- 24 NIV)

This is serious business! We must submit ourselves to each other. This does not mean we become doormats for each other; we must be careful how we use these words. These laws were not made by any man. There are God's laws. Let me make this clear: submission does not mean you use your spouse as a sex slave. Some spouses interpret this scripture in this way, and that is very wrong and very selfish.

Submission allows a wife to confidently follow her husband's visions and not be afraid to follow his lead. And Ephesians 5:23 makes it clear that a man does have responsibility for leadership in his home—but again, it is only as a leader that his wife submits to him, not as a tyrant or her superior.

God put this perfect plan in place for us to enjoy, not to use as punishment on each other. Husbands, you are head over your wife, but this does not mean you are going to be a taskmaster over her. It is very hard to be submissive to someone who treats you like a nobody. Remember your spouse is one of God's masterpieces, and God will hold you guilty.

Treating your spouse badly will not make you a bigger man or woman; it means you were not ready for marriage. Listen to the word of God and obey. This is God's business, not yours or mine. Be careful how you treat each other. The Bible is clear on every word. If you love each other, submission will be easy. Webster's Dictionary say to submit is to yield to power, will, or authority. We must be obedient to God's words if we want anything to work in our lives. Some people might think they can do it all by themselves, but without God, it can never work. It might look good at first, but things will change and all hell will break loose.

Make sure you listen to God's words and keep Him first in your marriage. 1 Peter 3:7, NIV says, "Husbands, in the same way be considerate as you live with your wives, and treat them with respect as the weaker partner and as heirs with you of the gracious gift of life, so that nothing will hinder your prayers." This is saying, husbands, God will not answer your prayers if you do not take care of your family. In a nutshell, both parties must be submissive to each other. Let me say, if you cannot submit to your spouse, then submit to God's words. The union of a man and a woman in marriage is a great mystery; it is a parable of the Christ and the church.

As a man and a woman marry, they become one flesh, so it is with Christ and the church becoming one body. Therefore, we must understand that our marriage is God's earthly image of His divine plan for mankind. In Ephesians 5:21-24, Paul is saying that the roles of husband and wife in marriage are not arbitrarily assigned, but are rooted in the distinctive roles of Christ and His church. Therefore, husband and wife must carefully study the word of God and apply it appropriately; then we will be able to adapt ourselves in the relationship God intended for Christ and His church.

A Christian husband should remember his role under God to provide spiritual leadership as a servant of his wife and family. Christ our king humbled Himself to be a servant among His disciples as an example for us to follow.

If your spouse should get ill, God forbid! Remember you are still one flesh, not only in the good times, but in the bad times too. This is where you take your stand as your spouse's protector and caring husband or wife and servant, not acting like a stranger or an enemy. It might be scary at first, but you should be supportive and show you understand. Helping your spouse through their illness can help them feel better sooner and have a better attitude. Dealing with illness is never easy, but we have a God we can call upon.

In some marriages, spouses get scared and change their minds when trouble comes in, and they end up leaving their matrimonial home without a comforting word. I must say, I am truly sorry for your experience, they did not love you in the first place and did not deserve you. But please remember all vengeance belongs to God; He will repay. According to Romans 12:19, NIV, God is the ultimate judge, and He will bring ultimate vindication. No evil will go unpunished, so as hard as it is, praying for your spouse, and forgiving them should be one of your main priorities, because there is no sin that will go unpunished.

Certainly, this is the time to assure your spouse of your love for them. Talk to them and remind them of the good times you have had together, or just sit quietly, depending on the situation. Everyone knows about the marriage vows "for better or for worse," but for some, these go out the window, forgotten in bad times.

In times of trouble, depression and hopelessness can creep into our marriage and go through the family. We must take precaution and be vigilant, relentless in prayer and fasting, before these even start showing their ugly heads.

Be careful who you talk to when your marriage is in trouble. Never go to someone who is not married or has never been married or someone who is divorced; it just might not be good for you at that time. Sometimes people are still hurting years after the end of a failed relationship or divorce, and they can't wait to unload on someone. Make sure you go to God first, then to men and women God would have you go to, experienced counselors in this field. As humans, when we are hurting and feeling low we do not need anyone to make us feel worse.

Please remember God can heal any broken heart. Psalm 34:18, NIV says, "The Lord is close to the brokenhearted and saves those who are crushed in spirit." Trust God and do the work by calling on Him and depending on Him. This emotional wound will be healed, you will be yourself again. Yes, my friends, our God can heal your broken hearts! You ask me how I know? I had no choice but to put everything in God's hands and to trust Him to heal my broken heart, and today I am very glad I did! God never fails, trust Him.

CHAPTER EIGHT
DATE NIGHT

"HONEY CAN WE GO ON A DATE?"

"Why would you want to go on a date, we are already married," her husband answered.

This was a conversation between two of my clients.

First let me say this: every couple should have a date night. Do not worry about money; date night can be in your living room and it can be any night. All you need just you two. Put a movie on, get something to drink, go walk in the mall eating an ice cream cone, take a long ride on the train, it doesn't matter—the most important thing is that you are together. Date night will give some spice to your marriage.

Remember when you were really dating and beginning to get serious about each other? Remember how special and good that felt? You would go to bed with each other on your minds. You couldn't wait to see each other the following day just to hold hands. It seemed like your hearts were beating at the same time. In those times, no one could point out any flaws about your partner to you, in your mind everything was perfect, and nothing else mattered.

Now, after two years of marriage, you just realize your spouse's nose does not look right anymore. You seem to actually irritate each other. All the things you could not see in the early days, you are seeing now. This is why you must keep romance alive in your Christian marriage! Keep doing the romantic things you enjoyed while dating, like sending love notes. Try to always admire your spouse and their achievements. Never allow this feeling to leave. When you talk about your spouse, there should be light in your eyes, and your heart should still have butterflies when you hear their name. This should never stop. Be adventurous in your marriage; there are lots of things you can do to keep the romance going.

My trusted friend, the late Deacon Cornell Hall, and I had a conversation about marriage one day. I asked him how long he had been married, and he said, "58 glorious years, ma'am." He said it with such happiness in his voice!

"How did you get through the hard times?"

He leaned his head and pointed his index finger on his right hand and said, "We go to God. We get in the word of God, ma'am, and ask him for help, and we leave it with Him."

"How do you stay around one person so long?" I asked.

"We spend a lot of time together getting to know each other, and learning to communicate with each other, and we listen to the word of God. Without the scriptures we could not make it, ma'am!" Then he said, "You must treat your spouse with kindness and love at all times. We must be honest with each other and talk about things, be quick to apologize. We should never allow our honeymoon to be over, and to be in a place of torment, that is not a marriage, and God will not be pleased with that."

All of us have weaknesses, but we have to learn how to over-look them. The Bible tells us that all have sin and fall short of the glory of God (Romans 3:23, NIV). That means *all* of us, so none of us can boast, saying how good we are.

After all the years, my friend said, he would do it all over again.

This was wonderful to hear. He said they never get bored of each other. Well done, my trusted friend. Rest in peace.

Couples who devote time together at least once a week have better communication with each other and even have lower divorce rates. If that is not enough evidence to start dating your spouse, I don't know what is.

Unfortunately, we get caught up with everything else and forget how important our spouse is. Children might come, and they are the love of our lives, but our spouse must not be put on back burner or feel lonely. Our spouse should always be our number one priority, not our parents, not our best friend, not our siblings. Yes, they all have their place, but your spouse most be in first place, never make your spouse feel less. This might surprise you, but they did not put themselves there, God did: "Husbands, love your wives, just as Christ loved the church and gave himself up for her" (Ephesians 5:25, NIV). Wives, your husbands were given the authority from God to be your priest, he must always be first, and nothing must take his place. Wives, you are the daughters of the King of glory our heavenly Father; we are strong and brave, and our Father as given us the faith we need. We are not alone; He is with us, so because of this, we can be the kind of Christian wives we are to be. Our Father Abba wants to show off in our marriage in a great way. We must obey the spiritual laws God had given to us, and know who you are in Him, if we want to have a happy marriage.

When you spent time with each other you get to learn your partner's likes and dislikes and know how to deal with them. In this way you will not say or do things they dislike and cause them to be hurt. I am not talking about just sitting at home, one reading, the other watching TV at all times—this is not spending time with each other or getting to know each other, because there is no talking! Something is wrong and must be fixed. Quality time together is actually talking, interacting with each other, like playing a game together and so forth, apart from those moments when we allow each other to have our own space.

Some spouses like to be surprised, so it would be nice to be spontaneous at times; this will make good memories for later. Marriage is a solemn commitment between a man and a woman, until death, and its hard work. You must be sure you are ready. Do not use your emotions or any obsessions you might have toward the one you are planning to marry; this is not love and will be a disaster.

If you see yourself in a vulnerable place, you must step back. This is not the time for marriage. I cannot emphasize enough that we must go to our Heavenly Father Abba with every decision we are about to make. It does not matter who we think we are; we just cannot do anything on our own. At first everything might look like it is working fine, but it will all go downhill—without God, we can do nothing! But we can do all things through Christ (Philippians 4:13, NIV). Celebrate your marriage with God's help every day, and make every moment you share count, because only you can make your marriage a happy one. Again, your marriage can be a dynamic relationship if God is in it.

This is my personal recipe. Try it, following the instructions carefully. You must put the work into this recipe for this sauce to come out just right.

Ingredients:

Prayer

God's Words

Patience

Forgiveness

Communication

Respect

Steps:

1. Both spouses are recommended to be working together in this kitchen.
2. Do not be afraid to put too much of any of these ingredients, this sauce can only get richer and better.
3. Not putting enough of any of the ingredients or leaving any of them out will completely spoil this sauce.
4. While making this sauce you must be able to taste it. The more you put in it, the better it will get.
5. Be relentless, and keep on cooking.

CHAPTER NINE
FOREPLAY

LET me say this to some of you husbands, you do not know what you are missing when you do not help your wives around the house. This has not been talked about a lot, but husbands, let me tell you this little secret! Have you ever heard your wife complain that you are not helping around the house? Well, she really would like your help, but more than anything, she enjoys watching you push that vacuum with your strong arms. She loves how you look standing at the sink doing the dishes. This is foreplay for her! Remember, foreplay is different from sex, but sometimes it can lead to sex, while other times just to be cuddled is great.

Some husbands might think everything to be done around the house is a woman's job, but this is not true! Either one of you can do it, make it easy on each other. Housework can be overwhelming at times, especially with a job and kids. Husbands, wives see you in a different light when you help around the house.

I understand that in the 1950s house duty was a wife's job, but not anymore! This is the twenty-first century, things have changed. Your wife is a helper: "And the LORD God said, it is not good that the man should be alone; I will make him a help meet for him"

(Genesis 2:18 KJV). God wants husbands to help their wives; she should not be burdened in any way, with house duty or anything else. This has been in the Bible all along, but some of us have not taken the time to read it. We have to be careful how we treat the responsibility in our homes. This can negatively affect other aspects of our marriage and cause major problems. Some husbands think if they do something in the home, they are just helping their wives; it is not their responsibility, and they see themselves as good husbands.

But our homes can be so much happier when we work together as a team! Spending quality time together is very good for your marriage. It does not matter what you do, this will help to keep your family as a unit. When we spend time together it tells a lot about us. It shows that we care about each other and we enjoy each other, especially if we are a blended family. That is another thing that can make marriage very unhappy—our kids can split us up in a minute, if we are not careful; they know how to manipulate us. There are some things to look for: sibling rivalry, seeking more attention, and a whole lot more, you must be sure if you want to do this. Each spouse must be able to discipline each other's biological child or children. When they see us as a team, they will back off. On the other hand, having a blended family can be a pleasant experience.

Putting your spouse first does not mean you do not love your children. We need each other for marriage to work God's way. In our marriage, no opinions matter except God's; this is why we must always invite Him into our marriage and everything else we plan to do. When we know our spouse loves us, we feel relaxed and secure with and around them. We might have problems with others, but with our spouse we are secure. Our families or friends may send negative signals about us but our spouse knows and loves us for who we are. May God speak to your hearts.

Wives, sometimes we can turn our husbands off by only seeing when they do something wrong. This might discourage them from doing anything, especially if she noticed something and talked about it constantly, this will make him uncomfortable.

Then there are the husbands who are lazy and do not want to do anything around the house. They know how, but because of the spirit of laziness, they are always relaxing. They need deliverance, haha!

Then there are some husbands whose wives have to tell what to do and they will, and they don't mind even if you tell them how to do it, but you have to know you are not bossing them around.

Another type will do everything halfway, and if his wife wanted to get someone to finish what he started, he will get mad.

Then another type of husband is on top of everything and makes sure everything is taken care of.

If you are a husband reading this book, examine yourself, and see where, with God's help, you can make improvement. May God continue to direct your footsteps and make you the kind of husband He wants you to be. Wives, you must remember your husbands are human, and please treat them like the man God had made them to be, and not something you can't stand to even look at. They were made by God and they are very important to Him. Be careful not to push them around and please treat them respectfully. Remember God eyes are on you, take care!

CHAPTER TEN
MY HEAD HURTS!

THERE IS ALWAYS something going on in our marriage to discourage us, but we have to remember that marriage was instituted by God and the enemy will always want to come in.

Always find out what is going on with your spouse. You must be honest to each other, there must be no assumptions or accusations made. We should listen to each other and try to understand the best way we can. We should be the only person our spouse can trust and confide in, with no reservations. You should be a safe place for each other. Our home should be a haven of peace with lots of love. We should be comfortable with each other and be able to share everything. This is the will of God for us, but unfortunately some of us take it lightly.

Because of this, some spouses suffer from lack of intimacy, and we are afraid to bring it up. This should never be. According to 1 Corinthians 7:2-5, NIV,

> But since sexual immorality is occurring, each man should have
> sexual relations with his own wife, and each woman with her own
> husband. The husband should fulfill his marital duty to his wife,

and likewise the wife to her husband. The wife does not have authority over her own body but yields it to her husband. In the same way, the husband does not have authority over his own body but yields it to his wife. Do not deprive each other except perhaps by mutual consent and for a time, so that you may devote yourselves to prayer.

This is why we must get things right by getting to know each other's sex language. This is every important to your marriage and it must be taken care of. If not, there will always be headaches.

As joint heirs of Jesus, we are to be mindful that we are in a war with Satan the enemy, and he will stop at nothing to add chaos to our marriage just because it is God's business, so pay attention to your dreams and visions. Remember anything our God can do, Satan has a counterfeit, so one of the things he will do is to send demons into your dreams to deceive you, as if they are married to you. Sometimes they even have sex with you, and the next thing you know your wives or husbands are turned off by you even coming near them.

I have spoken to wives who told me their husbands had this experience, and it brought lots of sorrow in their lives. The next time they wanted to be intimate with their wives, they found that they could not, until they got deliverance from God. This happens the same way with wives. These demons are known as spiritual husbands and spiritual wives. Let me say, they are commissioned by Satan to mess your marriage up. They deprive the married of sex. They steal affection and attraction for husbands or wives. At that time, everything and anything that can go wrong, will.

Illness, financial problems, and other troubles seem to appear everywhere, and you can't understand why this is happing. This problem of spirit husband and wife (spirit spouses), evil spiritual demons (incubi and succubi), is one of the greatest spiritual problems in marriages. Sad to say, there are vicious sexual spirits that are molesting and tormenting lots of people, married and unmarried. The unmarried might never get married unless they go through deliverance. If there is no deliverance through Christ Jesus, the marriage cannot be happy.

It is sad to say, there are lots of Christians that are experiencing this vicious attack from the enemy and are afraid to talk about it. Instead they suffer in silence.

This is why some spouses act so funny in bed. Some turn their backs. Some wives go to bed fully dressed—I mean, with a long-sleeved nighty buttoned up to the neck. They can't help themselves. Some husbands put the blame on their wives and depend on them to fix it. This makes a very unhappy home. They are always quarreling over some simple things that make no sense, and not getting to the real source of the matter. They are frustrated and do not know how to handle the situation. We cannot be afraid to fix this, by both spouses joining forces against the enemy for their deliverance.

Talking about this to our spouse should be a safe place, but unfortunately it is not so for some spouses. This causes some spouses to withdraw and not be transparent. As children of God, you must go to Him; if not, He will hold you both guilty. He is waiting for you; before the foundation of this world, He had given you the power. You have the power to move everything and everyone that wants to be a mountain in your marriage—they must be moved.

Intimacy was made by God for a man and his wife to enjoy. Marriage is holy and must be treated as such. There are no shortcuts.

You must invest in your marriage. God must be the head of your union. If not, all hell can and will break loose, and no one will be able to help. But when God is the head, the two of you can fight the enemy.

This is why you both must learn to fight fair and well, not hard. When there is a conflict, and they will come, you must remember your relationship with your spouse is sacred. How you speak to your spouse can make a big difference in the relationship, but actions in love make a bigger difference and even strengthen your bond with your spouse. Do not use your emotions. Healthy conflict is good. Try to talk about things before they get out of hand. Remember God is watching. There is nothing wrong with conflicts, but be mindful of the way you choose to deal with them.

Do not revisit past conflicts, for "Love keeps no record of wrongs" (1 Corinthians 13:5, NIV). Finally, love and submit yourselves to each other. This is God's command. Always fix your conflicts before nightfall. The Bible says in Ephesians 4:26, NIV, "In your anger do not sin, do not let the sun go down, while you are still angry." It is impossible to fall asleep angry when you have just held hands in God's presence; this intimate time will strengthen your marriage. This is why spouses must make a time for devotion in their homes every day. This will bring you closer together and will bring more love and affection in your marriage. You develop true intimacy with each other and with God. Enjoy your marriage, your union has been established by God before the foundation of this world.

Therefore, when you have a conflict, do not invite anyone in. If you find you don't know how to deal with a conflict, go to the Bible or seek spiritual leaders who can guide you God's way. You must have your eyes open. Sad to say, the enemy can use even the closest members of your family or your best friends to destroy your marriage. He is relentless and will stop at nothing to use and abuse us; he wants to see us dead out of Christ.

Saints of God, marriage was made by God, and it is holy, an example of our intimate union with God. As saints of God, we must live our lives in the knowledge of the fact that God has married us, both corporately as the body of Christ and individually as sons. I say sons, because there is no gender in Christ Jesus. He loves with all of Him, that He was willing to be beaten and be spit upon, even tortured by those notorious evil men. He was willing to go to the Cross just for us; to win our hearts back to Him, we must live our lives knowing that once we become a new creation in Christ Jesus, we are married to Him; we are in a covenant commitment to Him. Jesus said, "I give them eternal life, and they will never perish. No one can snatch them out of my hand." (John 10:28, NIV)

Husbands, you must love your bride like Christ loved the Church and gave His life for it. You must love your bride like your own body. Christ the bridegroom will be coming back for His bride the church, comprised of all of us who love and trust in Him, one day soon, and He wants us to be ready and waiting for Him. Are you ready? No one knows the time or the hour but our Heavenly Father Abba. Revelation 19:7-9, NIV says, "Let us rejoice and be glad and give Him glory! For the wedding of the Lamb has come, and his bride has made herself ready. Fine linen, bright and clean, was given her to wear." Fine linen stands for the righteous acts of God's holy people. "Then the angel said to me, 'Write this: Blessed are those who are invited to the wedding supper of the Lamb!' And he added, 'These are the true words of God'" (Revelation 19:9, NIV). The marriage supper of the Lamb will be a glorious celebration with Jesus Christ to his bride the Church. Hallelujah! My question is, will you be there? How do you treat your spouse? Do you anticipate seeing your love ones again? If your answers are in agreement with God's words, then I give our Heavenly Father Abba all the glory for you and pray you will continue to live for Him.

For those who are hoping to be married, you must understand marriage is God's business, and must be treated as such. I pray for everyone reading this book that it has helped in some way. I thank my Father Abba, for pouring into me, so I could pour into you. Enjoy your marriage.

Best
Sellers
Academy

This book was published with the support of The Legacy Project.
Do you have a book on the inside of you?
Let us serve as your midwives to help you give birth to your
international bestselling book!

Phone: 1-678-842-4346
Email: success@thebestsellersacademy.com
Website: TheBestsellersAcademy.com

www.ingramcontent.com/pod-product-compliance
Lightning Source LLC
Chambersburg PA
CBHW070134100426
42744CB00009B/1839